Insects and
Their Homes

This book has been reviewed
for accuracy by
Walter L. Gojmerac
Professor of Entomology
University of Wisconsin—Madison.

Library of Congress Cataloging in Publication Data

Oda, Hidetomo.
   Insects and their homes.

   (Nature close-ups)
   Translation of: Mushi no suzukuri / text by
Hidetomo Oda; photographs by Nanao Kikaku.
   Summary: Discusses how leaf-cutting bees, ants,
bagworms, and other insects make their homes.
   1. Insects—Habitat—Juvenile literature.
[1. Insects—Habitations] I. Nanao Kikaku (Firm)
II. Title. III. Series.
QL467.2.033513   1986   595.7'0564   85-28226

ISBN 0-8172-2528-5 (lib. bdg.)
ISBN 0-8172-2553-6 (softcover)

This edition first published in 1986 by Raintree Publishers Inc.

Text copyright © 1986 by Raintree Publishers Inc., translated by Jun Amano from *Insects and Their Homes* copyright © 1974 by Jun Nanao and Hidetomo Oda.

Photographs copyright © 1974 by Nanao-Kikaku.

World English translation rights for *Color Photo Books on Nature* arranged with Kaisei-Sha through Japan Foreign-Rights Center.

All rights reserved. No part of this book may be reproduced or utilized in any form or by any means, electronic or mechanical, including photocopying, recording, or by any information storage and retrieval system, without permission in writing from the Publisher. Inquiries should be addressed to Raintree Publishers Inc., 310 W. Wisconsin Avenue, Milwaukee, Wisconsin 53203.

1 2 3 4 5 6 7 8 9 0   90 89 88 87 86

Insects and Their Homes

Raintree Publishers
Milwaukee

◀ **A rose-cutting bee hides from the rain.**

This rose-cutting bee is one of the many leaf-cutting kinds, or species, of bees. Like other bees, it gathers pollen and nectar from flowers.

▶ **A rose-cutting bee cutting a leaf.**

Leaf-cutting bees have special long, sharp jaws. They use their jaws like scissors to cut the leaves of oak trees, roses, and dayflowers.

Insects are the most highly skilled architects and builders in the animal kingdom, except for people. Everywhere in nature there are insect homes—beneath the ground, in the bark of trees, on plant stems and leaves, under stones. Insects use the material around them—plant leaves, twigs, pebbles, dirt—almost as skillfully as if they were human carpenters, masons, or builders. Their tightly constructed, intricately designed houses can withstand sub-zero temperatures and hurricane winds.

Insects build homes for the same reasons people do. They need to have shelter from the weather and their enemies. And they need a safe place to raise their young.

It is the female leaf-cutting bee's job to find a suitable place to lay her eggs. She may decide on a hollow plant stem or bamboo stem, a hole in tree bark, or even an empty snail shell. The choice of home depends on the kind, or species, of bee and on the environment.

Often, the nest isn't the right size, so the bee alters it by lining it with plant leaves. Or she makes individual cells in the nest, using pieces of leaves or flower petals woven together.

The female leaf-cutting bee has sharp jaws, which she uses like scissors. Beginning at the edge of a leaf, she cuts out an oval or round piece. Next she rolls up the cut-out leaf and places it between her legs. Then she flies home to line her nest.

▶ A rose-cutting bee brings a leaf to her nest.

Leaf-cutting bees are similar to honeybees, but they don't live in colonies. When the female is ready to lay her eggs, she makes a nest all by herself.

◀ **A female bee carrying pollen to her nest.**

The leaf-cutting bee gathers pollen grains from flowers with the brush-like hairs on her abdomen and carries them back to the nest.

▶ **A nest in a bamboo stem.**

The female bee forms individual cells inside the nest by weaving pieces of leaves together. Oval-shaped pieces were used for the sides of this nest, and round leaves for the top and bottom.

When the female bee has finished constructing her nest, it has many tiny cells lined with leaves. Then the busy female sets out to collect food. She carries flower nectar back to the nest in her stomach. She collects plant pollen, which sticks to the hairs on the underside of her abdomen, and carries it home. She molds tiny balls of pollen and nectar and places one in each cell. Then she lays an egg in each cell.

Finally, the female bee seals the door to the nest, using chewed-up plant leaves and perhaps some grains of sand. When she is finished, the nest is so well built that no rain, wind, or enemy ants and beetles can get in. The eggs stay snug and safe inside the nest until they are ready to hatch.

▶ **A leaf-cutting bee larva.**

When an egg hatches, the worm-like larva begins to feed on the stored food in the cell. Soon it becomes a pupa and enters a resting stage. Finally, the adult bee emerges and bites its way out of the nest.

◀ **A chestnut leaf-cutting weevil.** This female chestnut leaf-cutting weevil is one of about ten kinds found in Japan. It is tiny—about a quarter of an inch long.

Leaf-cutting beetles and leaf-rolling weevils also use plant leaves to make nests for their young. Different varieties of beetles choose different kinds of leaves. Using their strong mouths, they bite into leaves or plant stems, cutting through the main veins. When the plant juices can no longer flow to that part of the leaf, the cut portion soon dries up. The female beetle then rolls up the dead leaf, using her legs.

The beetle begins to roll the leaf.

When the leaf has dried up, this tiny black beetle folds the two sides together and begins to roll it up.

The beetle uses all six legs.

The beetle uses three of its legs to hold the rolled leaf end. Using its other three legs, it rolls the leaf up.

The beetle bites the leaf.

Even though the leaf is withered, it is still hard to roll. The beetle bites the leaf to soften it.

▲ A leaf-cutting beetle's nest.

After the mother beetle finishes rolling its nest and laying its eggs, it flies away.

A beetle may roll up several leaf nests in a day. Usually, it takes about three hours to roll up a nest. In each leaf, the female beetle lays one to six eggs, depending on the species. She may deposit the eggs in the nest as she is rolling up the leaf. Or she may finish rolling the nest, then bite tiny holes in the outside and insert her eggs. Then the nest falls or is pushed by the mother beetle to the ground. The many layers of the nest cushion the fall. They also protect the eggs from enemies and bad weather. And they serve as a source of food during the second stage of the beetle's development. When the eggs hatch into larvae, they feed on the dying leaf nest. After each larva has grown sufficiently, it enters a resting stage, as a pupa. Within three weeks the adult beetle appears. It bites its way out of the remaining layers of the nest.

▲ **A beetle egg in a leaf nest.** The layered leaf nest provides food for the developing beetle. It also protects the beetle from enemies and the weather.

▲ **A skipper butterfly larva cutting a leaf.**
Skipper butterflies can be found all over the world. The females lay their eggs on the undersides of certain plant leaves, which the larvae will later feed on.

▲ **A larva cutting a leaf.**
The skipper butterfly larva cuts the leaf in the shape of a fan, leaving a small part uncut.

Butterfly larvae, commonly called caterpillars, often use leaves to make homes for themselves. Some houses are left open, others are closed up. Leaves may be rolled up by the caterpillar, or pulled together with the help of silk threads that the caterpillar spins.

Most caterpillars feed on plant leaves and stalks, and their mouths are well suited for chewing. The caterpillar of the skipper butterfly at the right is nibbling at the edge of a leaf. It cuts out a fan-shaped piece, leaving only a small part of the leaf uncut. Then it begins to fold the piece down by pulling on the surface of the leaf.

▲ **A larva folding down the leaf.** The larva tugs on the leaf's surface as it tries to pull down the fan-shaped piece.

▲ **A larva making a leaf nest.** The skipper butterfly larva spins silky threads again and again as it tries to pull down the cut leaf.

▶ **As the larva grows, it makes larger nests.**

The main activity of the larva is to eat and grow larger. As it grows, it leaves the old nest and makes a new one. Sometimes two or three nests can be found on the same leaf.

Like many butterfly and moth larvae, the skipper butterfly larva spins silk threads from its mouth. It attaches the threads to the fan-shaped piece of leaf and pulls on it. As the threads dry, they shrink and help to pull down the cut leaf. After spinning many threads, the caterpillar manages to fold the leaf in two. Then it spins more threads and attaches its house to the uncut portion of the leaf. The skipper caterpillar doesn't seal the ends of its house shut, as some species do. The tiny caterpillar stays in its house during the day. The folded leaf helps protect it from the hot summer sun and from its enemies.

◀ **A grove in autumn.**

Insects' homes may be located on the undersides of leaves, inside tree bark, or beneath fallen leaves. Insects build their houses in summer, since they know instinctively that cold weather is coming.

▶ **A grasshopper resting in its nest.**

These grasshoppers live in the warmer parts of Japan. They hide in their nests during the day and move about, searching for prey, at night.

This grasshopper makes its nest out of dried leaves. It pastes them together with a sticky substance that it secretes from its mouth. Grasshopper nymphs and adults both build leaf nests. They stay inside their shady homes, protected from the hot sun during the day.

▲ **A potter wasp making its nest.** The mother wasp busily builds a nest, using soil and her own saliva. She feels the edge of the pot with her antennae as the walls form.

▲ A mother wasp laying an egg.

The potter wasp lays one egg for each pot. She attaches the egg by a silk thread to the ceiling. That way it isn't disturbed when the paralyzed caterpillars stir around in the pot.

▲ A larva inside the nest.

When the larva hatches from the egg, it feasts on the stored caterpillars and beetle larvae. When it has grown enough, it stops eating and enters its resting, or pupal, stage.

Potter wasps use soil to form their tiny nests, which look like pots. They gather earth with their legs and jaws. Then they moisten it with saliva and pack it down with their tongues. As they build the sides of the nest, they use their antennae to feel the shape of the pot.

Then the female wasp hunts for beetle larvae and caterpillars, which the larvae will later eat. She stings her victims to paralyze them. Then she drags them to the nest and stores them inside.

The female lays one egg in each nest she has made. She hangs the egg from the ceiling on a silk thread. When the egg hatches, the larva will feed on the stored food.

The mother wasp seals the nest and soon the walls harden to clay. The little nest protects the larva, and later the pupa, snug in its cocoon, from the winter cold. In the spring, the adult wasp chews its way through the lid of the pot.

◀ **Black ants coming out of their nest.**

Certain kinds of black and harvester ants come out of their nests only once a year. In the fall, they break the seal of the nest and come aboveground to look for food.

Ants build some of the most elaborate houses in the insect world. The shapes of the nest and their locations vary. Some are attached to the trees, and others are hidden under tree bark. Many are underground. But they all have one thing in common—they are filled with many rooms and tunnels. This is because ants live together in large groups.

The female worker ants are the builders. They make many special rooms, or chambers, in the nest. Some chambers are used to store food. Others are nurseries for the eggs and larvae. And there is a private chamber for the queen ant. The rooms are connected by tunnels and passageways. Certain worker ants stand guard at the entrance to the nest to protect it from enemies.

▶ **A black ant gathering seeds.**
Harvester and certain kinds of black ants are very busy in the fall. They scurry about, looking for seeds to take back to the nest.

▼ **Seeds stored in the ants' nest.**
Worker ants prepare specialized chambers where the seeds won't spoil. The supply of seeds lasts the ants until the next fall, when they once again will come aboveground.

▲ A bagworm hanging from a branch.

During winter, bagworms hang from plants, rocks, and tree branches. This bagworm house is made to look like a dried-up tree leaf.

▲ A field in winter.

The moth larva called the bagworm carries its odd-looking house everywhere it goes. As soon as the larva hatches from the egg, it spins a house of soft, white silk. Then it secretes a sticky substance from its mouth and attaches bits of twigs, leaves, and bark to the outside. The house blends with the background, keeping the bagworm hidden from enemies. The bagworm uses its back legs to hold the house in place as it pulls itself forward with its front legs. When it finds a good place to eat, the bagworm parks its trailer-like home. Then it sticks out its head and begins to eat.

▼ **A bagworm moving in its bag.** Sometimes the bagworm moves around inside its house. The movement makes the bag swing back and forth.

▶ **A bagworm house in winter.**

Inside the bagworm house, the eggs or larvae are kept warm and dry. The bag keeps out the cold and snow.

◀ **A bagworm moth emerges.**

When the larva is full grown, it turns around inside its house. It then enters its resting, or pupal, stage. If a pupa becomes a male, the moth leaves the bag and begins flying around. If an adult female moth emerges, she stays in the bag.

Except for the adult males, bagworms spend their entire lives inside their homes. The adult female bagworm moth is wingless and never leaves her house. When a winged male finds her, the two mate and she lays her eggs inside the house. Most bagworms spend the winter in the egg or larval stage of their development. Their houses hang from branches or twigs, swaying in the cold winter wind. But, inside, the bagworms are snug and warm.

Let's Find Out

Do All Insects Make Nests?

Not all species of insects make nests for their eggs. Many newly hatched larvae must survive on their own. Female insects lay their eggs close to a suitable food supply. The larvae use their legs to move around looking for food.

▲ Dragonflies laying their eggs while flying.

Some dragonflies dive underwater to lay their eggs. Others fly above ponds, dropping their eggs in the water, one by one. The female dies soon after she has laid her eggs. Once the eggs hatch into nymphs, they are on their own. They search for food and hide from enemies on the pond's bottom.

Larvae Without Nests.

Insect larvae that don't have nests are in constant danger from enemies. Those larvae have different ways to protect themselves from attackers. Some have a body color that blends with their surroundings. Some have poisonous hairs. And some secrete bitter substances to discourage attackers. Generally, insects that don't make nests for their young lay more eggs than insects that do make nests. That way more larvae are likely to survive.

A dragonfly nymph catching its prey.

A measuring worm, which looks like a twig.

A butterfly larva with poisonous hairs.

This butterfly larva blends with the color of these leaves.

The Larvae Make Use of Other Insects' Nests.

Some larvae are actually cared for by other species of insects. The larvae of butterflies such as the black hairstreak secrete sweet juices which attract ants. Ants carry the larvae into their own nests and feed on the larvae's juices. The larvae survive the winter in the ants' nests and emerge from the nests in the spring to become adults.

◀ Black hairstreak larvae inside an ant's nest.

Let's Find Out

With What Do Insects Make Their Nests?

Most insects make their nests with the materials available around them—leaves, soil, and twigs. Some bees use pieces of tree bark, resin, or moss. Caddisflies, which live in the water, make their nests with small stones and shells. Some insects, such as butterflies, make nests by secreting substances, like silk. Some insects even lay their eggs in other insects' bodies and make their nests there.

● A wasp's nest made from chewed bark mixed with wasp's saliva (above). A caddisfly's nest made of small stones gathered on the river bottom (below).

Some Insects Use Substances from Their Own Bodies.

▲ Honeybees make their nests with wax secreted by the young worker bees.

▲ Spittlebugs make their nests by forming bubbles from their saliva.

▲ Spiders secrete a silky substance, which becomes strong when exposed to air, to form beautiful cobwebs.

Some Insects Make Use of Other Insects' Bodies.

▲ These wasp larvae feed on butterfly pupae.

▲ The wasps become adults inside the butterfly's pupal skin, and then emerge.

▲ A cuckoo wasp laying its egg inside a moth's cocoon.

See for Yourself.

Look for a bagworm hanging from a tree branch. Bring it home and cut open the bag, being careful not to injure the bagworm inside. Place the bagworm, without its bag, in a glass container. Put small pieces of colored paper and cloth inside the container. Soon the bagworm will begin to make a new bag, using the scraps of paper and cloth.

GLOSSARY

colony—a large group of insects which live together and depend on each other for survival, such as ants and some bees. (p. 7)

instinct—behavior with which an animal is born, rather than behavior that is learned. (p. 18)

larva—the second stage in the life cycle of insects that go through four stages of development: egg, larva, pupa, and adult. (pp. 12, 14, 15)

nectar—a sweet substance produced by flowers, eaten by insects such as butterflies and bees. (pp. 4, 8)

nymph—the second stage in the life cycle of insects that go through three stages of development: egg, nymph, and adult. (pp. 19, 28)

pollen—the tiny grains that contain sperm cells which fertilize the plant's eggs. (pp. 4, 8)

prey—animals that are killed by other animals for food. (pp. 18, 29)

pupa—the third stage in the life cycle of insects that go through four stages of development. During this resting stage, the body of the adult insect is forming. Often, the pupa is enclosed in a protective casing, or cocoon. (pp. 9, 12, 21)

species—a group of animals which scientists have identified as having common traits. (pp. 4, 5, 12)